THE RISE AND FALL OF THE PERSIAN EMPIRE

Ancient History for Kids
Children's Ancient History

BABY PROFESSOR

EDUCATION KIDS

Speedy Publishing LLC

40 E. Main St. #1156

Newark, DE 19711

www.speedypublishing.com

Copyright 2017

The Persian Empire was one of the great political successes of the ancient world. At its height it stretched from eastern Europe to western India. Let's find out about its rise—and its fall.

THE PERSIANS ARRIVE

The Persian people have a long and remarkable history, and have influenced the world in ways that continue today. They built a great empire, the largest and most powerful of its period, and they absorbed many other cultures and kingdoms.

Aryans

Three peoples, the Persians, the Medes, and the Aryans, all migrated south from the grasslands of Central Asia around 2000 BCE. The Aryans headed southeast into what is now India and Pakistan and conquered the people who were already there. The Medes and the Persians moved southwest, into Mesopotamia.

Mesopotamia, the land between the Tigris and Euphrates rivers in what is now Iraq, is often thought of as the "cradle of civilization". It is where the first cities in human history emerged. Learn more in the Baby Professor book Art, Religion and Life in Mesopotamia.

Tigris River

Elamite Rock

At the time, the biggest force in Mesopotamia were the Elamites. The Medes and Persians started conquering Elamite kingdoms, while at the same time absorbing Elamite customs and culture. But the process of moving from being a nomadic people, following the herds from place to place, to being a settled civilization with cities, farmlands, armies and a history, took well over a thousand years.

At this time the Persians were subject to the Medes. In 612 BCE, the Medes joined with the Babylonians to conquer the Assyrian Empire. Babylon took the more civilized areas to the south, while the Medes (and the Persians) claimed the wilder territory to the north, which was larger but not as rich.

THE RISE OF THE EMPIRE

In the middle of the sixth century BCE the Persians rose up in revolt against the Medes. They were led by a remarkable king we know as Cyrus the Great. By 550 the Persians had conquered their former masters.

Cyrus then attacked Lydia, in what is now Turkey. This was a very wealthy kingdom, and quite powerful. In the key battle, Cyrus had camel riders in front of his army. The horses of the Lydian cavalry did not know about camels, and were made afraid by their strange smell. The cavalry retreated, and the Persian army attacked and destroyed the Lydian forces.

Palace of Cyrus the Great

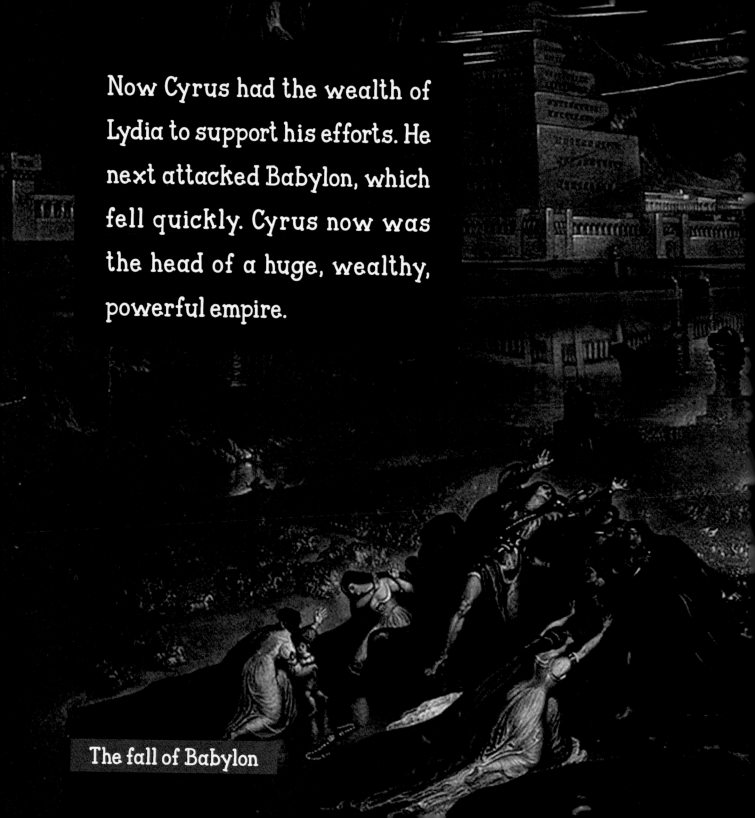

Now Cyrus had the wealth of Lydia to support his efforts. He next attacked Babylon, which fell quickly. Cyrus now was the head of a huge, wealthy, powerful empire.

The fall of Babylon

There were still raiders and threats from the northeast, the Persian home territory. Cyrus led his armies north into Central Asia, hoping to destroy those threats, but he died in battle in 530.

Tomb of Cyrus

Cambyses

Cyrus was followed by his son, Cambyses. He conquered Egypt in 525, but he seems to have been not as good a general or as smart a ruler as his father had been. The Egyptians hated him.

In 522 a cousin, Darius, started a revolt against Cambyses in Babylon. Cambyses died on his way to deal with Darius, and Darius became the next king of Persia. He was a great ruler and ruled from 522 to 486.

Army of Cambyses

GOVERNMENT

Darius had to deal with a huge empire. No king had ever had to manage so many people spread across so much area and so many cultures. He developed the government structures that helped the Persian Empire continue for over 200 years.

PROVINCES

Darius divided the empire into twenty "satrapies", or provinces. Each one was as large as a kingdom and was in charge of keeping order in its own area.

Palace of Darius the Great

Darius' Army

RIVALS

Since the satrapies were so large and had power to deal with rebellions within their borders, Darius knew the satraps, or governors, might decide one day to use that power to go against the central empire and himself. He took steps to keep the satraps under control and, if not loyal, at least cautious. Here were two of his measures:

CONTROL OF MONEY AND POWER

Except during emergencies, the tax collectors, treasury officers, and military leaders in a satrapy reported directly to the central government, not to the satrap. This made it much harder for a satrap to plan and pay for a revolution. When the satrap had local control, it meant there was already a revolt in progress and he would have his hands full trying to put it down.

Persian Soldiers

Persian Warriors

LISTENING

The king had agents called "The King's Ears". They would visit the courts of the satrapies to see and hear what was going on, and then would report back to the king. These agents were highly trained-and highly feared.

KNOWLEDGE

One of the biggest problems for a huge empire in ancient times was how to know what was going on far from the capital, and how to be able to send orders quickly to respond to emerging events-a flood, a famine, or a force of invading troops. Darius had troops of messengers on fast horses, and relay stations. One rider would ride all day, changing horses at the stations, until he was too tired. Then he would hand off the message to the next rider, and the message would go speeding on its way.

Persian Cavalier

Medes and Persians

The Persians built a system of roads to help the message riders, and to make it easier for armies to get to where they were needed. One of these roads, the King's Highway, had over 100 way stations with fresh horses, inns for travelers, and patrols to defend against attacks from bandits. It stretched over 1500 miles from Susa, the Persian capital, west to Sardis in what is now Turkey. A message carried along the King's Highway could get from Sardis to Susa in just a week.

DIVERSITY

In one major way, Darius was different from all rulers before him in Mesopotamia. Rather than forcing all nations and peoples to become like Persians, upsetting people and leading to costly revolts, Darius practiced tolerance. There were certain things, like paying taxes and honoring the king, that everybody had to do. But they were free to keep their own customs and, for local communication and business, their own languages and laws.

Darius even allowed the Jews, who had been a captive people in Babylon, to return to their homeland and go back to worshiping and living in their traditional ways.

RELIGION

When the Persians arrived in Mesopotamia, they and the Medes believed in multiple gods, mainly related to the weather and the seasons. Around 600 BCE Zoroaster developed a new religion, which we call Zoroastrianism after its founder. This religion saw a mystical battle between the forces of goodness and light on one side, and the forces of chaos and darkness on the other. People would be judged after death on how well they supported the forces of goodness while they were alive.

Zoroastrian Symbol

The kings took a role within religious practice as the visual representative of the forces of good. It was a great honor even to be allowed to kiss the king's sandal, and it was dangerous to look at his face without being invited to. The court had complex rituals that built up a sense of the king's power and importance, but that also isolated him from contact with most of his people.

THE FALL OF PERSIA

Even the best-organized kingdom needs a king who is good at what he does, and has a good dose of luck. Darius was followed by Xerxes, another good and strong king; but when he died in 464 BCE there was no strong and lucky leader to follow him. The satrapies became more powerful and more independent. They made their own treaties with other nations, and sometimes went to war with other satrapies, without considering what the "great king" might want. Egypt and other conquered areas were frequently in revolt.

Xerxes I of Persia

Achaemenid Tombs

Trade, and therefore tax collection, faltered as wars and disruptions became more frequent. This led to higher taxes and a more repressive government ... which in turn led to even more rebellions and disruptions.

It became clear that the Persian giant had great weaknesses. Finally Alexander the Great of Macedonia invaded Persia with a small, but very capable, army. He managed to conquer Persia, destroying their armies although heavily outnumbered, by 331 BCE. Persia became part of a great Greek empire.

Alexander the Great

The Palace of Ardashir, Sassanid Dynasty

Persia rose again, as the Sassanid kingdom, around 200 CE. The Sassanids continued until about 650, when they were conquered by the Arab armies of Islam.

THE INFLUENCE OF PERSIA

Although Persia was now under Arab rulers, it passed on its culture to the Arabs. Much of what we think of as Islamic customs and traditions have their roots in the Persian world.

Map of Persia

Persian City

Persia arose as an independent body again around 1500, and continues to this day as Iran. Iranian culture treasures and celebrates its past of great empires and magnificent cities.

EMPIRES RISE AND FALL

There have been great empires in all parts of the world except Antarctica. Read about the rise and fall of other kingdoms and empires in Baby Professor books like A Quick History of the Mayan Civilization, The Assyrian Empire's Three Attempts to Rule the World, and The Byzantine Empire.